Animal Groups

Alan Trussell-Cullen

 Nelson Thornes

First published in 2007 by Cengage Learning Australia
www.cengage.com.au

This edition published in 2008 under the imprint of Nelson Thornes Ltd,
Delta Place, 27 Bath Road, Cheltenham, United Kingdom, GL53 7TH

10 9 8 7 6 5 4 3 2
11 10 09 08

Animal Groups
ISBN 978-1-4085-0058-3

Text by Alan Trussell-Cullen
Edited by Kate McGough
Designed by James Lowe
Series Design by James Lowe
Production Controller Hanako Smith
Photo Research by Gillian Cardinal
Audio recordings by Juliet Hill, Picture Start
Spoken by Matthew King and Abbe Holmes
Printed in China by 1010 Printing International Ltd

Website www.nelsonthornes.com

Acknowledgements
The author and publisher would like to acknowledge permission to reproduce material from
the following sources:
Photographs by Auscape International/ Jeff Foott, p. 5; Getty Images/ The Image Bank, p. 7/
Stone, pp. 13 top, 14 bottom; NewsPix/ Andrew Henshaw, p. 15 top; Photo Edit/ Michael
Newman, p. 14 top/ Myrleen Ferguson Cate, p. 15 bottom; photolibrary.com/ OSF, front and
back cover, pp. 1, 6, 10/ Ifa-Bilderteam Gmbh, pp. 3, 12 top/ Animals Animals/ Roger De La
Harpe, pp. 4, 11/ Franc Krahmer, p. 8/ Naylor Lawrence, p. 9/ Andrew Plumptre, p. 12 bottom/
Jeff Lepore, p. 13 bottom.

Animal Groups

Alan Trussell-Cullen

Contents

Chapter 1

ANIMAL GROUPS

A lot of animals live in family groups.

Wildebeest live in groups.

A group of wildebeest is called a **herd**.

a herd of wildebeest

Dugongs live in groups called herds, too.

a herd of dugongs

Dugong Facts

1 Dugongs cannot see very well.

2 A baby dugong gets milk from its mother.

Chapter 2

ANIMAL MOBS

Meerkats live in groups.
A group of meerkats is called a **mob**.

a mob of meerkats

Meerkat Facts

1 A mob can have five to 30 meerkats in it.

2 All the meerkats in a mob
look after the baby meerkats
when the mothers are eating.

Kangaroos live in groups called mobs, too.

a mob of red kangaroos

Kangaroo Facts

1 Red kangaroos look for food at night.

2 Not all red kangaroos are red.
Some are blue-grey.

Chapter 3

BIRD AND FISH GROUPS

Some birds fly in groups.
A group of birds is called a **flock**.

a flock of birds

Some fish live in groups.
A group of fish is called a **school**.

a school of fish

Bird and Fish Facts

1 Birds can see and hear well, but they cannot smell well.

2 Fish have no eyelids, so you cannot see when they are asleep.

INSECT GROUPS

Some insects live in groups.
A group of bees is called a **swarm**.

a bee hive

Bee Facts

1. Over 60000 bees can live in a big **hive**.

2. All the bees have to work to look after the hive.

11

Chapter 5

ANIMAL GROUP FACTS

FACT 1: A group helps make the animals safe.

FACT 2: The big animals in this group look after the little animals in the group.

Running Words 106

FACT 3: The animals in this group
look after the baby animals.

FACT 4: Not all animals live in groups.
A lot of animals live alone.
The bear is an animal that lives alone.

Chapter 6

PEOPLE GROUPS

A lot of people like to be in groups, too.

We work in groups at school.

We play in groups of friends.

We like to go out in little groups.
We like to go out in big groups, too.

Not all people
like to be in groups
all the time.

A lot of people like
to have time alone.

Glossary

flock a group of birds

herd a group of animals, such as dugongs or wildebeest

hive a place where bees live

mob a group of animals, such as kangaroos or meerkats

school a group of animals, such as fish

swarm a group of animals, such as bees

Index